Wind Resistance

Karine Polwart is a multi-award-winning Scottish songwriter and musician, as well as a theatre maker, storyteller, spoken-word performer and published essayist. Her songs combine folk influences and myth with themes as diverse as Donald Trump's corporate megalomania, Charles Darwin's family life and the complexities of modern parenthood. She also sings traditional songs and writes to commission for theatre, animation and thematic collaborative projects. Karine is five-times winner at the BBC Radio 2 Folk Awards, including twice for Best Original Song.

In association with the Royal Lyceum Theatre and Edinburgh International Festival 2016, Karine wrote, musically directed and performed *Wind Resistance*, her critically acclaimed debut work for theatre. A poetic meditation on midwifery, ecology, sanctuary and solidarity, it combines elements of memoir, essay, myth, sound art and song. *Wind Resistance* won the Best Music and Sound Award at the Critics Awards for Theatre in Scotland, 2017.

D1448596

KARINE POLWART

Wind Resistance

For Rosie
Remember the geese!
Karip x

ff

FABER & FABER

First published in 2017
by Faber and Faber Limited
74–77 Great Russell Street
London WC1B 3DA

Typeset by Country Setting, Kingsdown, Kent CT14 8ES
Printed in England by CPI Group (UK) Ltd, Croydon CR0 4YY

A CIP record for this book is available from the British Library

ISBN 978-0-571-34585-4

2 4 6 8 10 9 7 5 3

Wind Resistance, a Royal Lyceum Theatre Company production in association with the Edinburgh International Festival, supported through the Scottish Government's Edinburgh Festivals Expo Fund, was first performed at the Royal Lyceum Theatre, Edinburgh, on 4 August 2016.

Writer, Composer and Performer Karine Polwart
Director Wils Wilson
Dramaturgy David Greig and Liam Hurley
Visual Designer Camilla Clarke
Sound Designer Pippa Murphy
Lighting Jeanine Byrne
Movement Janice Parker
Videography Sandy Butler
Stage Management Jessica Ward
Live Sound Ben Seal and Mark Whyles

Thanks also to the wider Royal Lyceum team, especially Alex McGowan, David Butterworth, Dawn Taylor, Ian Gibson and Ruth Butterworth

Text Adaptation Consultancy Liam Hurley

A companion album exists, entitled *A Pocket of Wind Resistance* (Hudson Records, 2017). Many of the tracks complement chapter headings of the same name within this text.

Author's Note

This publication attempts to capture something of a live work on the page. I'm primarily a singer, songwriter and storyteller. I've never written a show for theatre before. *Wind Resistance* combines elements of writing about landscape and ecology, local history and memoir, traditional storytelling and song. To me, it's more of a poetic essay or musical meditation than it is a play.

It's personal stuff too, in that it connects my home, my children, my neighbours, my ancestors, and my values. In making the show, it wasn't my intention to craft a stage piece that might be readily adapted by others. That's true also of this text (though please feel free to try).

The songs I weave into the piece are traditional or older public domain works, as well as my own original writing. Full credits are in the Appendix. These songs have an integral role in the content and cannot be swapped out for others. *Wind Resistance* itself is, in part, the digging into and unfurling of the back-story to one of these songs, 'Salter's Road'.

As sole performer of the piece, I move between speech and song, sometimes in the course of a single phrase. As I do so, I accompany myself on a variety of instruments, including guitar, tenor guitar, shruti box, sansula and Apogee Duet midi-controller.

In addition to songs, I underscore live spoken word and prerecorded narration. I interact also, vocally and spatially, with prerecorded sound and with short abstract film sequences, which hint at birds and bogs.

In the absence of visceral sound, music, space, movement, and other visual cues to distinguish different iterations of my voice, I offer a structural and spatial guide to the layout of the text.

My live speech and storytelling (my 'lines') sit thus to the left of the page.

SONG
Song lyrics are indented in italics.
Sung lines and rhythmic incantation
are italicised in the body of the text.

A thread of third-person historical narrative frames the whole piece. It maps the story of Will and Roberta Sime, a young couple who lived as farmers in my rural home landscape during the early years of the last century. In performance, Will and Roberta's story is, for the most part, prerecorded in my voice. It sits in a sonic space that's distinct from my live storytelling and singing voice. For clarity and ease of recognition, I situate their story thus on the page.

Notes on staging, light,
movement and sound
are over here. Often
I use first-person
description, as this is
not a guide to future
production, so much
as a record.

The Set

a Victorian tangle
of roots and gridlines
test tubes and vials
vases and glasses
bog cotton, heather
bracken and bone
a barn owl
a school desk
a Captain's chair

ACT ONE

ACT TWO

WIND RESISTANCE

Act One

ONE: ALL ON A SUMMER'S EVENING

*Near darkness. Dawn
chorus, A hypnotic,
looping chime.*

SONG
*As I was walking ower yon hill
All on a summer's evening
There I spied a bonnie lass
Skippin' barfit through the heather*

*And oh but she was neatly dressed
She neither needed hat nor feather
She was the queen among them a'
Skippin' barfit through the heather*

*An older woman's
voice speaks.*

'Roberta was the love
of his life.'

'She was definitely
head-over-heels in love
with my incredibly
unattractive
grandfather, skin and
bone (*Laughs.*) but
adorable . . . a kind,
kind man.'

*She wore a goon o' bonnie blue
Her petticoats were a pheasant colour
And in between the stripes were seen
Shinin' bells o' bloomin' heather*

3

Older woman's voice.

'Granny Roberta was
not allowed to marry
this man.'

'Old Grumpa, if he
wasn't marrying
Roberta, he was
marrying no one.'

Oh dear lass, wad ye gang wi' me?
Wad ye gang wi' me and leave your heather?
Silks an' satins ye shall wear
If ye'd gang wi' me and leave your heather

Older woman's voice.

'Roberta was the love
of his life. Roberta was
the love of his life.
Roberta was the love
of his life. Roberta was
the love of his life.'

In the final week of May 1919, Will Sime's last lamb is
born. He strides out from Currie Lea past Crichton, and
the tall Scots pines. The sky melts . . .

amber, cherry pink and violet . . .
as the ground levels on to Fala
Moor and the Forth Valley opens
up a thousand feet below him. He
traces the line of the Salter's Road
down to the sea. The wind blows
up, and he hears her, before he
sees her, his Roberta, her clear
true voice lilting through the
heather in amongst the larks for
the first time since he left that

4

　　　　　desert war. There she sits with her
　　　　　narrow back to him, her black
　　　　　hair tumbling down her spine, her
　　　　　bare feet dangling in Fala Flow.

The story of Will and Roberta is our story.

TWO: THE MOOR SPEAKS

The light lifts.

If you leave the Edinburgh city by-pass at Millerhill
Junction and head south towards Jedburgh, the first
village you pass through is Pathhead, Midlothian, which
is where I live. Two miles further down the A68 is the
village of Fala and just beyond there, a way-marker
points west to Brothershiels Farm.

You can rumble up the pot-holed track past Fala cemetery,
between narrow hedgerows. Then through the new steel
gate and under the buzzing power lines that wind down
into The Borders, before skirting a copse of oak, larch
and birch, and new-growth spruce plantation in behind.

Then. Suddenly. Just beyond the trees. The whole sky
expands.

I open my arms.

This is Fala Moor, my local peat bog.

There's a wonderful expression in the Welsh language,
about rushing, hurrying through space. Anyone who
knows me will tell you I do this a lot. I'm a fast-talking,
fast-walking wifie! It translates into English as 'holding
your breath in your fist'.

I tighten my hand.

At Fala Moor . . .

*I unclench my fist and
blow hard across my
hand.*

. . . I can feel my whole palm open. And it opens into a
landscape to the North that follows the line of the Old
Salter's Road down to the Forth and across to Lower
Largo Hill in Fife. On a crisp winter day you can see
beyond that as far as the snowcapped Sidlaws and
Cairngorms.

To the North-East, the volcanic hump of North Berwick
Law defines the East Lothian coast. And beside it the
white glimmer of the Bass Rock, the world's largest
colony of Northern Gannets.

From the East you can trace inland along the scarp of the
Lammermuirs to Soutra, upon which stand the twenty-
six turbines of the Scottish Power Dun Law wind farm.
I find them very beautiful.

Just below the brow of the hill is the old tumbledown
seventeenth-century chapel of Soutra Aisle. And beneath
that, the buried remains of what was the medieval Soutra
Hospital.

The Pentland Hills, in the West, frame an enclave of tall
Scots pines at the moor's edge. And just out of view are
Crichton Glen and the farm of Currie Lea, where Will
and Roberta lived.

Then the panorama returns full circle to Castle Rock,
Arthur's Seat and North.

The heart of Fala Moor is a small lochan called Fala
Flow. It doesn't look like much, but it sustains the whole
wetland.

If you lob a pair of hydrophones in there, waterproof
microphones, there's a lot going on underneath the
surface. And this is true of the whole landscape.

Listen. That sound, a bit like a grasshopper or a tiny guiro, is a queer wee insect called a water boatman. It's only two millimetres long, but relative to its size, it's the noisiest creature on earth! And it lives right here at Fala.

Listen again to what's underneath your feet:

> the crunching upon gravel
> the crinkling in the rushes
> the snapping of the muirburn
> and the shlooping of the bog

In summer, Fala Moor is peppered first with the white tufts of bog cotton before turning to a blaze of dense, springy purple heather.

It's a landscape which rewards the widest possible gaze, and also the narrowest possible focus. On your hands and knees, or hunkers, it's dense and colourful. The bog mosses are soft and squidgy. My kids love to bounce on them! I love to lie on them. And they have such magical names:

> *sphagnum palustre*
> with its wee lime green and copper stars
> *sphagnum auriculatum*
> like clumps of rhubarb and custard
> the vibrant cherry red
> of *sphagnum magellanicum*
> and *hylocomium splendens*
> otherwise known as glittering wood moss.

These lush mosses are just the visible outer lining of a raised peat bog ecosystem that's evolved over millennia at Fala Moor, upon beds of decaying, organic matter, layers of life and death, and life and death.

In Scotland, our peat bogs are our largest and most efficient natural carbon store. And in this respect, they're like the lungs of our land.

I camped out one night at Fala Moor with the sound designer for this show, who's called Pippa Murphy. We were woken at around four a.m. by this sound . . .

A zip fastens.

Actually, that's Pippa getting back into her sleeping bag after hitting 'record'! Hear that?

A lone whistle.

That's a Golden Plover, a wee wading bird that takes its name from the Latin *pluvia*, to rain. And that?

A harsh craik.

That's a Red Grouse. In Scots it's called a Moorcock, and it has this unmistakable call: go back – go back – go back. You'll hear it.

Go back – go back –
go back.

And there, that's one of the most spectral sounds of the moor, the Curlew.

Currrr-lee-ew.

And then finally . . .

The sound rises.

Bringing up the dawn, dozens and dozens of skylarks.

SONG
Up and awa and awa wi' the laverock
Up and awa and awa in the morning
Up and awa and awa wi' the laverock
Up and awa tae the hills for me

THREE: LISTENING TO BIRDS

*Dawn chorus
disappears.*

'Mum, I think I can talk to birds.'

It's my son, climbing into bed first thing one morning.

'Wow,' I reply, 'That's cool! What do you say to each other?'

'Well, it's kind of hard to tell you, Mum, because, well . . . well, we don't talk human.'

And he proceeds to make these lovely soft cooing noises. 'Oh, is that pigeon? Do you talk to pigeons, love?'

'Yup,' he says. 'Actually, I talk to lots of different ones, but mostly pigeons and crows . . . cos they're very like people.'

'And what happens when you talk?' I ask.

'Well, I just listen to what they're saying . . . and then I say something back.'

'Is it like when Harry Potter talks parcel-tongue to the snakes?'

'Exactly,' he says.

SONG
*Up and awa and awa wi' the laverock
Up and awa and awa in the morning
Up and awa and awa wi' the laverock
Up and awa tae the hills for me –*

FOUR: LARK IN THE CLEAR AIR

The Scots word for lark is 'laverock'. They're ground-nesting birds whose survival depends upon their ability to become instantaneously invisible!

I snap my fingers.

A wee bit like Harry Potter himself.

If larks could transform into people, like selkies do when they leave the sea, then I reckon they'd look a wee bit like my Granny Polwart did, in her knee-length tweed and her beige Marks 'n' Spencer's cardigans. She liked to go unnoticed. And so do I. Indeed, one of the main reasons I escape so often to Fala Moor is to disappear, and to listen to something other than the sound of us.

But there's this brilliant dichotomous aspect to skylarks, which I can relate to. I can transform, on occasions such as this one, from a solitary moor-walker into an excited, blethery performer. And just like me, when those larks take off they totally go for it. They do that unmistakable helicopter style hovering thing . . .

My right hand floats up slowly.

Fluttering up and up on an invisible shaft of air – singing, and singing . . .

My gaze follows my hand.

Until they become, in the words of the Borders poet James Hogg, 'a little musical star on the breast of heaven'.

I stretch to my highest.

These audacious bursts of song are for courting, and for marking territorial boundaries. They're also a defensive mechanism. What precedes lift-off is often a low sleekit scarpering on foot, well away from their vulnerable cupped nests in the ground.

This decoy come-and-get-me tactic works well against overhead predation by the likes of merlins or buzzards.

But it's totally useless in the face of a fifteen-tonne combine harvester.

Widespread winter-crops farming on the edges of Fala Moor is a disaster for skylarks. It means they're unable to feed on open stubble in the cold months, because the grain grows too high. And in the spring, when they're trying to establish their fragile nests in the fields, the crops are being cut down.

As a result, skylarks are a red-listed endangered species in the British Isles. They seem plentiful up on this bog land, and yet they're under existential threat.

Sometimes what we need to know about a place and what's evolved to live and thrive there is embedded in language itself. In Gaelic, the word for skylark is 'fosg'. It means, literally, open space . . .

> *I reach my arms straight ahead as if about to swim, then sweep them in a broad arc.*

Including the space that's above us.

> *I raise my arms slowly, deliberately above my head.*

When I go to Fala Moor, I get filled up with space. I need it for my own wellbeing just as much as those larks do. Clear, open space is what defines Fala Moor. It's what defines moors everywhere.

SONG
Dear thoughts are in my mind
and my soul it soars enchanted
as I hear the sweet lark sing
in the clear air of the day.
For a tender beaming smile

to my hope has been granted
and tomorrow she shall hear
all my fond heart longs to say.

I will tell her all my love
all my soul's pure adoration,
and I know she will hear my voice
and she will not answer me nay.
It is this that gives my soul
all its joyous elation
as I hear the sweet lark sing
in the clear air of the day

June 1919: just a month since
they found each other again in the
heather at the Flow. The bride,
Roberta Sime, takes the hand of
her new husband Will. Her family
is not in attendance. And she
recalls how her own mother had
told her, long before the war took
Will away, that a better man was
meant for her. But she had waited
for him nonetheless.

Dear thoughts are in my mind
and my soul it soars enchanted
as I hear the sweet lark sing
in the clear air of the day
in the clear air of the day

Water. Water boatmen
chirrups.

FIVE: LABOURING AND RESTING

> *A swelling drone.*
> *Hummed reprise of*
> *'Skippin' Barfit . . .'*

All the way home!

> *Crying, flying geese.*
> *Looping, cascading*
> *guitars.*

Snaefell – Skaftafell

skein, skein

Tasilaq – Kulusuk

skein

Torshavn – Kvivik

skein, skein

Scrabster – Kinloss

skein

Strathbeg – Leven

skein, skein

Aberlady

Fala

Fala

In September, the geese snake in across the Firth of Forth, from their summer nests in Iceland and the coastal cliffs of Greenland, clattering and honking in their ever-shifting skeins.

My garden is a flight path. I watch. I listen.

The outstretched wing-tips of each migrating goose create an upwash, a pocket of wind resistance for the bird tucked in just behind and below. These neuks of ease, these aerodynamic sanctuaries, cut the drag by up to 65 per cent. It's a wonder. And it's also a gale-bitten struggle to sustain co-operation.

Every goose takes a turn:

> stepping up – falling back
> labouring – and resting
> stepping up – falling back
> labouring – and resting

> > *The wind whirls. The sound of geese rises and falls.*

Like sky-borne socialists, no lone bird bears the brunt of the wind.

> *holding on, holding on*

It's a gorgeous symbiotic dance:

> stepping up – falling back
> labouring – and resting
> stepping up – falling back
> labouring – and resting

> *skippin' barfit through the heather*

> > *A hum, a hymn, a wind turbine.*

> > *The sound disappears.*

Two thousand four hundred pink-footed geese winter on the moor at Fala Flow. The pink-foots of Fala used to roost on the coast at Aberlady, until Second World War weapon testing harried them inland.

They remember this.

Geese pass information from generation to generation, creating a kind of collective memory. And so the descendants of those World War Two birds settle still at Fala Moor.

And it's on account of these hardy birds, with their pink feet and pink beaks, that my local moor is designated an SPA at European level: a Special Protected Area. In the UK, Fala Moor is also a SSSI, a Site of Special Scientific Interest, both for the geese and for the rare peatland habitat that holds them.

I watch those geese fly in to Fala, in a bluster, and I see a small clutch lose the skein, a disconnected cluster. And I know in my bones: they won't make it on their own.

Guitar underscore.

But I don't just worry about those geese. I worry about us too, how readily we get lost to our own selves, separated from the people and places that might offer us protection, and who need us to protect them.

I worry about the weather that's to come.

SIX: TYRANNIC MAN'S DOMINION

SONG
Now westlin winds and slaughtering guns
bring autumn's pleasant weather
The moorcock springs on whirring wings
amang the bloomin heather
Now waving grain, wide o'er the plain
delights the weary farmer
And the moon shines bright as I rove at night
to muse upon my charmer

The partridge loves the fruitful fell
The plover loves the mountains
The woodcock haunts the lonely dell
The soaring hern the fountain
Through lofty groves the cushat roves
the path of man to shun it
The hazel bush o'er hangs the thrush
The spreading thorn the linnet

Shooting grouse is a leisure that's exclusive to the wealthy so our moors assume the shape of their desires. If you look up Fala Flow on Google Earth, the land's a charred patchwork and a plume of smoke still smoulders in the north-east corner.

The moorcock loves fresh heather shoots to feed upon but needs old heather cover when it's time to rest and mend. And so heather moors are burned back, to privilege the moorcock, cos it's worth it: it gets five-star treatment.

At Fala, in 2000, the fiery butts of heather kept on burning. They couldn't be contained. The blaze ravaged underneath the surface of the bog. It isn't clear if it will ever be the same . . .

Thus every kind their pleasure find
The savage and the tender
Some mortal join, some leagues combine,
some solitary wander
Avaunt away, the cruel sway –
Tyrannic man's dominion
The sportsman's joy, the murdering cry,
the fluttering gory pinion

Tyrannic man's dominion: Robert Burns wrote this in 1783. And now our dominion extends to the wind, the 'fosg', the space above the moor itself.

In recent years, my local council ruled against a turbine application on the edge of Fala Flow. And it wasn't for the pink-foots or the peat bog, but to spare the view from the windows of our cars as we drive the A68.

And it makes me angry that my local council doesn't take a view that goes beyond what can be seen. And I worry and I wonder how we plan to power our world, and, look at me with all my gadgets and my gear.

But the moor talks back to me . . .

it being the lungs of our land
and the larks in the clear air sing
in the sky that they command
and my heart has room to grow
where I can open up my hand

this space to be
in which to love and be loved
what's that worth to me?
what's that worth to us?

But Peggy dear the evening's clear
thick flies the skimming swallow
the sky is blue, the fields in view
all fading green and yellow
Come let us stray our gladsome way
and view the charms o' nature
The rustling corn, the fruited thorn
and every happy creature

We'll gently walk and sweetly talk
till the silent moon shines clearly
I'll grasp thine waist and fondly pressed
swear how I love thee dearly
Not vernal showers to budding flowers
not autumn to the farmer
sae dear can be as thou to me
my fair my lovely charmer

Will watches the pink-foots twisting overhead towards the moor, as the swallows abandon the eaves of Currie Lea for the warm skies of Africa. He recalls his own journey south four years before. The troop train. The boat to Egypt.

Autumn would mind him always of feverish nights in those scorching sands.

For Roberta, during that early autumn of 1919, after the war, after the wedding, it was the time of quickening, the time before seeing, when she just knew, when she placed Will's hand gently, wordlessly, upon her belly.

SEVEN: A PLACE TO REST AND MEND

To understand and appreciate this landscape that I live in and love is to look beyond what can be seen.

Five hundred and seventy-four seeds were found up there in the heavy clay. Three hundred and seventy-two of them were black henbane, a plant so deadly that one whiff could knock you over. Henbane yields three key chemical compounds:

>*hyoscamine* – which is used nowadays to treat stomach conditions

>*atropine* – which is used to regulate heart rate

>and *scopolamine* – a common sedative and anti-spasmodic.

There were ninety-four seeds of hemlock too, the plant that bumped off Socrates in Ancient Athens. Hemlock contains conium, another sedative. And, curiously, one of the only creatures to have evolved immunity to its toxin is the skylark.

A hundred and eight opium poppy seeds were unearthed, from flowers that were shown to have been cultivated at Soutra itself.

Together, henbane, hemlock and opium were key ingredients of early anaesthetics.

These plant remains were discovered during a meticulous medico-archaeological dig, a tender hand-sifting of soil beneath the grounds of what was the medieval Soutra Hospital. It stood twelve hundred feet above the Forth Valley on the edge of the Lammermuirs. And it was the highest ever known monastery or hospital in all of the British Isles.

> *When the plagues and the soldiers*
> *marched up The Royal Road*
> *North – South – East – West*
> *You dressed your wounds in sphagnum*
> *and you drank from the flow*

The hospital was sited just off the old Royal Road that ran north and south between Scotland and England more or less parallel to the A68 today. It was known then as the House of the Holy Trinity, a settlement of Augustinian monks, described in a fifteenth-century supplication to the Holy See of Rome as 'near a public way where there are often fierce winds'.

Soutra Hospital was founded in the twelfth century on a charter to serve the poor, the infirm, the aged and the sick, all those who could not help themselves. And in this respect it's the seed of our modern-day universal health systems and services.

The Augustinian priests were expressly forbidden from practising midwifery. It's clear though, from further botanical traces and from foetal and stillborn remains at Soutra, that pregnant women were attended, if not by the priests themselves, then by spaewives, older women with skills as midwives and nurses, and reputations often as seers.

Locally sourced juniper berries were identified, as well as ergot, a fungus that lives on grain. Both juniper and ergot stimulate the uterus, and they've been used throughout history as abortifacients, which is why gin is known as 'mother's ruin' and ergot, in German, as 'wombgrain'. Ergot was used also as a means of expelling the placenta after birth and for stemming post-partum haemorrhaging. Indeed the derivative compound, ergomitrine, is still used in modern labour-ward drugs today.

Alongside the seeds at Soutra were shards of human bone. The priests, and possibly also the illicit midwives, were surgical pioneers as well as herbal healers. And there's no doubt they would have gathered from Fala Moor, down below Soutra Hospital, those magically named sphagnum mosses:

   Sphagnum palustre
   Sphagnum auriculatum

Bog mosses can absorb up to twenty-five times their own mass, making them perfect as wound dressings. And they've been used in this way across time and space

   from Kashmir to the Eastern seaboard of Canada,
   from Lapland to Ypres and the Somme.

> *I hum a pipe retreat*
> *march. We hear*
> *shouts, gunshots.*

At night, Will still hears the
artillery fire. The burning of flesh.
The breaking of bone. The
crashing, the smashing of earth
and stone.

But it would not be the worst
sound he'd hear in his life.

I wail. I keen.

EIGHT: ANGELA

*An old school bell
rings.*

In the Primary One school photograph I'm wearing a red
hand-knitted jumper under a grey pinafore and I'm
clutching my hands between my knees. On my feet is a
pair of navy-blue Clarks kickers. My mother has clearly
cut my hair.

To the left of the frame, a wee girl sits pert and upright,
like a meerkat. She has elbow-length blonde hair clipped
back with pins and she's wearing classic 1970s NHS specs
that make her eyes look huge.

She's the first girl I meet on my first day at school, when
we're forced to line up in twos by the double doors and
our mums stand quietly weeping in the playground.

She tells me her name is Angela.

A few weeks later, she visits our house a mile up the back
road, and we play, illicitly, on the roof of my next-door
neighbour's piggery. Our Sindy dolls enact Wonder
Woman stunts into the trough below.

Later still, Angela squeezes herself into a calf-length black
tube of lycra and perfects the kohl rims around her eyes.

And on Tuesday nights, at the Denny High School Youth Club disco, whilst I'm dancing awkwardly around my electric-blue snakeskin stilettos Like a Virgin, Angela has the wind in her sails.

> *I turn out my arms*
> *and spin slowly.*

She's conjuring the spirit of Morrissey and Ian Curtis and Robert Smith.

> *I pick up speed,*
> *dancing in an arc.*

In the spring of our final year at high school, Angela recognises something of herself in the wild bespectacled redhead we watched spinning and flailing her arms around on *Top of the Pops* last night.

That Fairground Attraction singer, Angela tells us, is from Irvine. And though we're not actually sure where that is we know in our hearts that it's a place exactly like here. And Eddi Reader, in Angela's eyes, is evidence of hope.

In September 1999, at Stirling Royal Infirmary, Angela gives birth to her first child, a wee boy. I've no idea if she ever gets to hold her son, because she's rushed to Glasgow Southern General, and three days later she dies as a result of post-partum complications.

Of course, it's no consolation at all to Angela's family that she's one of only a handful of women in Scotland to die in or as a result of childbirth that year. And there's no solace either in knowing that if you go back – go back – to the 1920s, when Angela's grandparents and mine were born, and before we had yet imagined our National Health Service into existence, close to one in twenty-five women in Scotland died each year in labour or shortly after giving birth.

SONG

*I'm going home
and I'm going home soon
beo beo
I'm going home
and I'm going home soon
beo beo*

*To where a boy at the window
is opening up his wings to the world
I'm gonna be there, when he takes to the air
I'm gonna watch them unfurl*

*Oh beo, beo, beo
Oh beo, beo, beo
Oh beo, beo, beo, beo
Oh beo beo*

*I'm going home
and I'm going home soon
beo beo
I'm going home
and I'm going home soon
beo beo*

*To where a girl at the window
is opening up her heart for the first time
I'm gonna be there to keep it from care
I'm gonna hold it in mine*

*Oh beo, beo, beo
Oh beo, beo, beo
Oh beo, beo, beo, beo
Oh beo beo*

> *I continue to sing
> quietly.*

Roberta clasps her hands over the swell of her apron and stands watching Will from behind the narrow scullery window. He nuzzles the good mare and coaxes her and her young one into the stable for the night, with a low canted murmuring, the closest he ever gets to singing.

I'm going home, I'm going home,
I'm going home, I'm going home, I'm going home,
I'm going home, I'm going home,
I'm going home, I'm going home, I'm going home,
I'm going home, I'm going home,
I'm going home, I'm going home, I'm going home,
I'm going home, I'm going home,
I'm going home, I'm going home, I'm going home,

To where a boy at the window
is opening up his wings to the world
I'm gonna be there, when he takes to the air
I'm gonna watch them unfurl

Oh beo, beo, beo
Oh beo, beo, beo
Oh beo, beo, beo, beo
Oh beo beo

Act Two

NINE: EVERGREEN

The pink-foots were already in at the Flow and the weather was on the turn. It grew brisker and darker each day in the copse at the edge of the moor. And all the creatures of the moor were making ready for winter.

A wee bird was hopping about one morning in the trees up there. In fact, it was a robin, foraging for nuts and seeds.

There was a fluster and a gang of boys came tearing up the track from Fala village. Suddenly, one of the boys stopped. He'd spied the robin among the trees, and, who knows what made him do it? He picked up a stone and threw it at the bird.

There was a terrible crack as the robin's wing broke.

The boy was terrified by his own self, and ran helter-skelter back down the track to Fala, with his pals.

The robin groaned and tucked his wing up behind his back. He knew right away in his bones and feathers that if he didn't find a place to rest and mend then he wouldn't make it through the weather that's to come.

The North Wind rustled through the undergrowth.

The first tree the robin met was the fine, elegant Birch stretching her limbs in the autumn light.

'Dear Birch,' he cried softly. 'A boy has broken my wing with a stone and I can't fly. If I don't find a place to rest and mend then I won't make it through the weather that's to come. Can you help?'

The Birch peered at the robin. 'Ocht, it's one of you songbirds. You're never done chittering from dawn till dusk. You're such a nuisance. There's no room for you here. You'll have to move on.'

And she went back to her stretches.

The robin felt stung. Song was his nature. And the wood and the whole moor rang with it.

The North Wind whistled through the branches and the robin shuddered. He hopped on until he met the Oak.

'Dear Oak, a boy has broken my wing with a stone and I can't fly. If I don't find a place to rest and mend then I won't make it through the weather that's to come. Can you help me?'

The Oak scoffed. 'You pathetic wee bird. You think you can come stealing acorns from under my nose, leeching off the rest of us here in the wood, and expect my sympathy? There's no space in my branches for thieves or beggars. Away you go and fend for yourself!'

The words landed on the robin, as the stone had. For the acorns, once fallen, were no more the Oak's than anyone else's. They were a bounty for all the birds and creatures of the wood.

The North Wind whistled through the leaves then. And the robin shuddered again and went on through the trees. By the edge of the copse, where it meets the gale-bitten bog, he met the beautiful feathery Larch.

'Dear Larch, a boy has broken my wing with a stone and I can't fly. If I don't find a place to rest and mend then I won't make it through the weather that's to come. Can you help me?'

The Larch recoiled. 'Who are you?' she hissed. 'I've never see you here before, little bird! Get out of my garden and go back to wherever you came from! There's no room here for strangers.'

The robin wept. For this was his wood. And he was tired and sore.

But as he wept, a voice spoke from above.

'Wee bird, what's the matter?' The robin looked up. It was the Spruce. 'A boy has broken my wing with a stone,' said the robin, 'and I can't fly. I know if I don't find place to rest and mend then I won't make it through the weather that's to come. The Birch called me a nuisance. The Oak called me a thief. And the Larch refused me as a stranger. I don't know what to do.'

'Then rest in my branches,' said the Spruce. 'There's plenty room and my needles will keep you warm.'

Then another voice spoke. It was the tall Scots Pine. 'I can shelter the Spruce from the worst of the wind,' he said, 'and together we'll keep you dry.'

The robin was amazed.

And then a third voice, a soft voice, spoke. 'I have beautiful dark berries for you,' she said. 'I can feed you all winter long.' And it was the Juniper.

And so the Spruce and the Pine and Juniper looked after the robin through the frosty months that followed. And in the spring, he was rested and mended and flew off singing into the woods.

But that is not all.

The North Wind had witnessed it all. And he was furious.

'I am the weather that's to come,' he bellowed, as he whipped through the wood at Fala Moor. And when he met the Birch and the Oak he tore their leaves from their branches. And when he reached the Larch he stripped every needle from her limbs, and hollered. 'You denied the robin when he needed you most. From this moment onwards,' the North Wind declared, 'when the weather turns, and the geese are in at the Flow, the Birch, the Oak and the Larch will stand naked and shivering through the cold months of winter. But the Spruce, the Pine and the Juniper? They'll keep their coats.'

And this is the old Scots Traveller story of how the spruce became evergreen.

Wind, bleating sheep.

One bitter March evening, Will and the mare drag in a fine, heavy stump of fallen pine from the copse at the edge of the moor.

He sets to it in the barn after supper, while Roberta sits by the stove, humming to herself and conjuring delicate bonnets for the bairn to come.

When he's done filing and smoothing and oiling the wood to a gentle shine, he wraps his handiwork in an old blanket and tiptoes in through the scullery door. 'Close yer e'en,' he whispers to her, and she lays aside her lace for a moment as he sets it at her feet. 'There ye are,' he says, as he whips away the cloth.

It's the bonniest crib she's ever seen.

Larks sing.

TEN: SMALL CONSOLATION

She saw something flash out the corner of her left eye,
just beyond the kitchen window, and then heard a small,
dull thump.

A guitar loops.

She set down her cup and hauled herself out of the chair,
squeezing her belly awkwardly around the table's edge.
She wrapped on a shawl against the spring air and
waddled to the back door for the first time that morning.

For days now, she'd watched the pair dart in and out
the eaves, and glancing up she saw at once: the nest was
gone.

Her eyes flickered to the ground. It was scattered in the
gravel, pale grey tufts of down spinning towards it in the
breeze.

Oh my God. The fledglings.

Five of them: four utterly broken, smashed up wee
dinosaurs. And worse yet: one twisted, but still alive, its
heart continuing to beat, an impossibly huge, red heart
in such a tiny, scrawny body.

And then it was over.

She stood there and wept, wept for the fragility of life.
Tumbling out her own unspoken fears for the creature
she carried within herself.

She wept for the incomprehensible effort of that same
swallow pair – how they'd flown . . .

A rippling, ascending
melody.

From the Orange River delta in South Africa, across the Congolese rainforest and the desert skies of the Sahara. Up to two hundred miles a day.

Then whipped in behind the Atlas Mountains of Morocco, before skirting the eastern edge of Spain: Almeira, Valencia, Barcelona.

Traversed the Pyrenees, and the full length of France and England, only to see their nest, their brood, fall from the worn stippling of a Midlothian farmhouse wall. For a second year in a row.

Ocht, the poor swallows. They're the birds, in old Nordic lore, who attended Christ on the Cross, crying:

Svala! Svala!   *Svala Svala!*
Console! Console!   *Console! Console!*

They're the birds of consolation itself. But there was none to be had.

She lumbered to the shed, fished out a handsaw and a hammer and some nails. She hoicked a battered crate on to the bench.

It was a labour, right enough, reaching across the expanse of her own midriff to secure the joints and measure the angle of the roof.

It was a ragged affair, yes, but it was a birdhouse nonetheless.

A sanctuary.

SONG
Have you ever held something
until your hands were aching?
And then let it go and watched it fall
and listened to it breaking?
I have held back time and tide

when all the world was plenty
but now my hands are open wide,
open wide and empty

For every breath that leaves me now
another comes to fill me.
For every death that grieves me now,
I swear the next will surely kill me.

For those borders crumble every day,
the faultlines are showing
and all I thought was here to stay
slowly is going

History abandons us
and we're holding on, holding on
to nothing but dirt and dust
we're holding on, holding on
and we're holding on, holding on
and we're holding on, holding on
and we're holding on, holding on
and we're holding on, holding on

while those borders crumble every day
the faultlines are showing
and all I thought was here to stay
slowly is going

A note of discord,
a drone.

One morning, she stopped singing.
Will had barely noticed until then
how much the house and yard at
Currie Lea was filled with the
melody of her – scattering seed for
the hens – weaving at her lace
bobbins – or stirring broth over the
stove. Her song was a fact, like the

weather, or the larks announcing the dawn. Now her swollen body pulsated with low moans.

After supper that evening, Will walked out again to the Scots Pines on the moor's edge and recalled Roberta's voice floating in from the Flow less than a year before.

ELEVEN: WHITE OLD WOMAN OF THE NIGHT

I used to live a little further down the A68 from Pathhead, in a farm worker's cottage just over the brow of Soutra Hill. To my delight, the ramshackle outbuildings of the steading housed barn owls, one of my favourite creatures.

In Scots, the generic name for owls is 'hoolets'. It's an onomatopoeic reference, though barn owls don't hoot at all. They screech, like banshees.

In Gaelic, they're wonderfully named: 'cailleadh oidhche gheal', the white old woman of the night.

A Doppler monitor.

A barn owl portends a birth: a little girl, or otherwise, a labouring and labouring.

Heartbeats.

And so when the pulsing within me grows steady and insistent every breath is hauled up from a deep, dark place that I didn't recognise . . .

And when we judder down the pot-holed farm track to meet the Old Royal Road that takes me to the Maternity Unit at Borders General Hospital . . .

And when that white old woman of the night, the 'cailleadh oidhche gheal', catches the car's headlights and skims the bonnet with her wings, I remember the old stories, and I cant the names of girls:

> *Frankie Rosa*
> *Eva Cora*
> *Ada Isa Belle*
> *Frankie Rosa*
> *Eva Cora*
> *Ada Isa Belle*

> *Beo beo, bonnie bonnie beo*
> *Beo beo bonnie bairn o' mine*

> *I love ma little girlie*
> *your hair is nice and curly*
> *I love you, I love you*
> *I love you cos you're mine*

You can believe in portents, as you will. I can tell you that I did not give birth to a girl that night.

> *I love my little laddie*
> *You're just like your daddy*
> *I love you, I love you*
> *I love you cos you're mine.*

It's a marathon to reach the maternity unit from the A&E doors. I stop a dozen times on those stairs whooshing, breathing in half the sky. I'm far too busy occupying my own body to be terrified.

> *Deep breaths, heavy*
> *breaths.*

The midwife who books me in is nearing the end of a long night's shift. And she looks spent. Her first words on my arrival are to her colleague.

'An elderly primigravida,' she says, meaning that I, like the barn owl, am an old woman, or at least, at the age of thirty-six, old for a first-time mother. She glances at me, and makes some kind of assessment of my resilience in that moment. Without any kind of physical inspection she says, 'Aye, you'll be a while yet, love.'

'No,' I say. 'I don't think I will.'

'Ach, that's what all the new mums think, love!'

That midwife knew many things that I didn't, and she'd seen and heard things I hadn't. And besides she was bone-tired, and she needed a cup of tea. And I was in this strange bewildering place in my body. So what could I possibly know?

'Just settle yourself in to the room.' She nods around the birthing suite. 'I'm away to put the kettle on. The next shift arrives in ten minutes.'

Barely a minute elapses and I'm as sure as I've ever been about anything. 'This baby is coming,' I hiss. 'She needs to get back in here. Right now.'

She comes in. (*Sighs.*) 'OK, up you get and we'll take a look.' And I lumber on to that metal bed.

'Ohhh.' Her whole tone was altered. 'Oh my goodness, you're maybe nine and a half centimetres here, this baby is wanting out.' And then she looked me directly in the eye and said, very clearly, 'There's a hand. It's a compound presentation.'

'A what?'

'It's trying to come out like a wee superman, love, with its left hand on its head! You'll need to stop pushing right now.

'Stop!'

*Momentary silence, the
rush of blood, a heart
monitor racing.*

Two full days Roberta lay in
labour in the back room at Currie
Lea, wailing now beyond any
beast in the field, her new
mother-in-law tending to her.

Will could hardly bear it.

The first consultant marches in, in a great whirl of panic,
and he tries to move my desperate-to-be-born but
resolutely stuck baby, within me, with his bare fist and
arm, without any explanation, and without even so much
as a gas-and-air. And a sound emerges from my belly,
which I wouldn't have believed a human being could utter.

I wail. . . .

Still, that baby will not be moved.

I become aware then of white-coated bodies circling and
muttering and pointing. 'Hang in there, lass,' the new
midwife whispers in my ear, 'And dinnae push. Dinnae
push ony mair. There's a good lass.'

Every evolved cell in my body wants to push. Of course it
does. I have to rally my mind against the will of my belly.

*Henbane, Hemlock, Opium, Juniper, Ergot
Henbane, Hemlock, Opium, Juniper, Ergot*

'They're calling in the anaesthetist, so we can have
another try at moving the bairn.'

Pause.

'And they'll be making the operating theatre ready too.'
She nods to the cluster of coats at the door.

A deep drone.

35

TWELVE: SPHAGNUM MASS FOR A DEAD QUEEN

SONG

Queen Jane lay in labour
full six days or more,
till the women grew weary
and the midwives gave o'er.
They sent for King Henry
to come with great speed
To be with Queen Jane
in her hour of need

King Henry came to her
and he sat by her bedside
Saying 'What ails thee my Jeannie?
What ails thee my bride?'
'O Henry, O Henry,
do this one thing for me,
rip open my right side
and find my baby'

'O Jeannie, O Jeannie
that never will do.
It would lease thy sweet life
and thy young baby too'
She wept and she wailed
and she fell into a swoon
They opened her right side
and her baby was found

I wail. Drones build.

Sphagnum palustre
Sphagnum auriculatum
Sphagnum cuspidatum
Sphagnum magellanicum
Sphagnum capillifolium
Hylocomium splendens

36

*I incant a liturgy of
mosses, a sphagnum
mass, keening and
wailing over swelling
drones and a choir of
overlapping voices.*

*Sphagnum auriculatum
Sphagnum cuspidatum
Sphagnum magellanicum
Sphagnum capillifolium
Hylocomium splendens*

*Whispering, whispering,
wheeshing, hushing,
then a bright, dreamy
bed of sound emerges.*

The epidural to my spine, when it comes, is an
unbelievable blessing. In the glorious numbness that
ensues, another obstetrician arrives. He looks like he
could deliver lambs on a hillside in a blizzard, and maybe
he has. He talks to me like a person. And as the Caesarean
team hover like hawks in the hallway, tenderly he eases
back in the hand of that nearly born superman.

Over the next fifteen minutes, the midwife cajoles me like
a rugby coach through the immense waves, which still
judder through my body. I can't feel them at all. I can
only see them, like craggy spikes on the monitor screen,
with its wire attached to my stomach. She hollers as they
rise: 'Go on, lass! Push into it! This is the time!'

*needles and wires
and knives and stitches
and beeps and clicks
and hums and pips
and pulses and drones and drips*

ergomitrine
oxytocin
prostaglandine
diamorphine
pethidine
bupivocaine
methergine
syntometrine

needles and wires
and knives and stitches
and beeps and clicks
and hums and pips
and pulses and drones
and drips.

A drone re-emerges.

SONG
Well that baby was christened
the very next day
while his poor dead mother
a-mouldering lay.
Six men went before her
and four more travelled on
while loyal King Henry
stood mourning alone

He wept and he wailed
until he was sore
saying 'The flower of all England
will flourish no more.'
He sat by the river
with his head in his hands
Saying 'My merry England
is a sorrowful land'

Dawn chorus lifts.

At 9:35 a.m. on the 29th May, 2007, my son Arlo was
born at Borders General Hospital. I'm clear now, in a way
that was opaque to me in the animal process of birthing
itself, that we made it, me and my son, with thanks to all
those souls who went before us, the ones whose fingers
and femurs lie in clay on Soutra Hill, alongside the ergot
and juniper and the magical opiate potions of those
monks, and those impermissible midwives.

The name Arlo is from an old Germanic word for
fortified place, a place you fight for, a place you defend.

I wrote this song for him just a few months after he was
born.

SONG
This weary Earth we walk upon
She will endure when we are gone
While kingdoms come and kingdoms go
Rivers run and rivers flow

You know I don't believe it's true
That in this world there's nothing new
For darling you have just begun
Rivers flow and rivers run

And if the river should ever run dry
somewhere the rain will still fall,
still fall from the sky

When I'm beguiled by the fear
that Darker Days are drawing near.
My darling, you seduce the sun
Rivers flow and rivers run

And if the river . . .

This wounded Earth we walk upon
She will endure when we are gone
But still I pray that you may know
How rivers run and rivers flow

And if the river . . .

So I cross my heart and hope to live
Just long enough that I can give
It all to you, my darling one
Rivers flow and rivers run

Arlo is nine years old now and, like many Scottish kids of his age, he's football daft.

When I began high school in Denny, Stirlingshire, girls were not allowed to play football. I used to sit in my morning registration class in what was the Home Economics block and gaze wistfully towards the Technical Department, where girls were not allowed to make things from wood or metal either.

I could let that stuff go. But the football really bugged me.

And so, in the pre-summer term of 1983, when it came time to register for the annual S1 and S2 seven-a-side football competition, me and my pal Gillian Rutherford decided enough was enough. We put together an all-girl squad for the first time.

We were both mad into football at the time. Specifically, we were fans of Aberdeen FC. Aberdeen, after all, was on its way to the final of the European Cup Winners' Cup.

It was a legendary squad under legendary manager Alex Ferguson. Defending the net was Scotland goalie Jim Leighton. In defence was the big ginger Alex McLeish. Me and Gillian had, by some miracle, secured the autographs of both players, who happened to be sitting in the concourse café of Aberdeen railway station as Denny High School volleyball team arrived on the train for a national schools' match in the city.

We couldn't believe our luck as they signed our John Menzies paper bags.

One of the understated lynchpins of the Aberdeen first team at the time was full-back Stuart Kennedy. Kennedy picked up a brutal knee injury in the second leg of the semi-finals, which left him unfit to play in the big match. In fact, he'd never play a professional match again.

But when it came time to pick the squad for the final, on May 11th 1983, against the mighty Real Madrid, Ferguson chose Kennedy for the bench. It was a nod of respect for Kennedy's role in taking Aberdeen to the final, and an intimation of Ferguson's evolving managerial philosophy:

Teams win games.
Squads win titles.

> *Sound of an excited crowd. I don headphones and pick up a dictaphone.*

OK, you have to imagine me in a sheepskin coat, like Archie Macpherson or Dougie Donnelly:

'It's match day at the Nya Ullevi Stadium on the biggest evening of Aberdeen Football Club's history. Seventeen thousand Dons fans have travelled to Gothenburg. It's a carnival atmosphere here in Sweden.'

> *A whistle blows, a football is kicked.*

'Six minutes in and the corner swings in for Aberdeen. Alex McLeish is making a late run from the back and he heads it into the penalty area. And the goal is given!'

> *Crowd cheers.*

'It's Black! Young Eric Black! What a tremendous start for Ferguson's men.'

> *I interject.*

It was a short-lived after glow. Six minutes later, Jim

Leighton brings down Santillana just outside the six-yard box and Juanito levels from the penalty spot.

Crowd groans.

'Three minutes to go here in Sweden and Alex Ferguson is making one final substitution. Oh, it's controversial! Yes. John Hewitt is coming on in place of Aberdeen's only goal-scorer, Eric Black.'

*Ninety-minute whistle
sounds.*

'Twenty minutes into extra time and that's a good ball in from Peter Weir. And now Aberdeen are making the break. And Hewitt's waiting in the middULLLLLL!'

Crowd roars.

I take off headphones.

In our separate Stirlingshire living rooms, Gillian and me, we can't believe it. In the 112th minute of the game, late substitute John Hewitt scores the winning goal.

The Real Madrid coach, Alfredo Di Stéfano, would say afterwards: 'Aberdeen have what money can't buy: a soul, a team spirit forged in the family tradition.'

In 1986, Ferguson was lured from Aberdeen to Manchester United, where he coached for twenty-six years, becoming the most successful British football manager of all time.

Ex Man U striker Ryan Giggs recalls, 'It would be in the middle of training – and he'd stop . . . and he'd say – "Right, all of you look up to the sky." And we'd look up, and these birds would be flying in a V-shape, and he'd say: "See that? That's teamwork."'

Erstwhile Ryder Cup Captain Paul McGinley invited Ferguson to mentor the European squad at Gleneagles

Golf Course in 2014. I don't know if you recall, but the press image that captures their moment of glory shows them laughing and pointing to the sky.

> *I stoop down and*
> *point upwards.*

'When we won, this perfect V of geese flew right over our heads and over the clubhouse,' McGinley explains. 'It was a phrase we used throughout the week: remember the geese.'

> *My arms draw the V of*
> *a skein above my head.*

Remember the geese.

> *A swelling drone.*
> *Swirling geese.*
> *Looping guitar.*

FOURTEEN: REMEMBER THE GEESE

> *All the way home!*   (ho-ome)
> *Mile and miles and miles*   (ho-ome)

I watch and wonder at the geese as they fly up the line of the Salter's Road to Fala Moor each autumn.

> stepping up – falling back
> labouring – and resting

The skein is their refuge. And so is the moor itself.

The sanctuaries we've conceived and wrought for one another, from the medieval Soutra Hospital to our modern maternity wards and operating theatres, they're like the outstretched wing-tips of pink-footed geese, neuks of ease and care, places to rest and mend. And proof, for now, that our gaze expands, as it does at Fala, way beyond our individual selves.

So far, we're holding on to what we've made.

holding on, holding on

But the weather grows darker and brisker every day and the wind is fierce and unrelenting.

We are each other's wind resistance, a human skein.

And we're not going to make it on our own.

> *A stark wind. A distant*
> *keening purl of birds.*

FIFTEEN: MOLLY SIME'S WELCOME
TO SALTER'S ROAD

On the third afternoon, the last blizzard of the year hurtled in over Soutra, smothering the tiny, white flowers at Strawberry Hill. Will lambed all night amongst the bleating flock till his knuckles were raw. Only one was lost to the frost.

A wet-nurse was called in to attend the bairn, while her mother lay like a fresh-cut barley field. Her wailing was at an end, yes. But her breath was as parched and brittle as muirburn. And the accelerating silence that followed was unbearable for Will.

The snow melted *(Underscore resumes.)* the day after his daughter arrived. He left the ewes to their own work and sat beside his Roberta that evening, stroking her pale, clammy hand.

44

SONG

She was waiting for a boy
in her corduroy britches
driving on a Clydesdale
like her father once had done
from Mutton Hole to Preston Hall
through all the dells and ditches
and an avenue of burly beech
that reach towards the sun

For miles and miles and miles she'd roam
down Salter's Road to Fala Dam
and all the way home
for miles and miles and miles she'd roam

She was waiting for a boy
in his trews of navy cotton
Something she had half-forgotten
is as clear as water now
The horseman's only daughter
takes the Friday boat to Bergen
And the waves swell like a barley field
that's ready to lay down

For miles and miles and miles she'd roam
down Salter's Road to Fala Dam
and all the way home
for miles and miles and miles she'd roam
down the spine of the St Lawrence
to Kirkwall's stony shore
The old north wind
gathers her into his arms once more

> *Silence.*

She hadn't stopped bleeding since
the bairn left her. And she bled
and bled till the oak floorboards
of the room were sodden with the

life of her. There was no doctor
or midwife worth sending for, no
opium or ergot to ease her. It was
just one of those things. Some
make it. And some don't. Like
yowes. Will would never
comprehend it.

The good society family who'd
disowned Roberta on account of
her love of this quiet horseman
sent a carriage for her body. Will
wound her in sheets himself,
swaddling her like a bairn. And
though he'd never know where
they laid her in her grave, he'd
bury her in his own way,
somewhere deep inside himself.

He took an axe to their bed that
evening and tore every board from
the back-room floor. He stacked
them in a pyre and threw on the
bloody linen and blankets. Then
he struck a match . . . and let the
world burn.

> *A fire begins to*
> *crackle.*

> *A gentle guitar pattern.*

Will ties up the horses and takes
his daughter's hand. Molly. She's
his shadow, and her mother's.

I knew that wee girl Molly, Will and Roberta's daughter.
By then, she was an old woman, my neighbour on the old
Salter's Road that runs from Pathhead down to the Forth.

On the last evening of her life, I visited her at Liberton Hospital in Edinburgh with my son Arlo. He ran the full length of the ward shouting: 'Molly! Molly!'

Molly Kristensen, the only daughter of Will and Roberta Sime. I wrote this song for her . . .

Will and Molly wander the fields all the way from Currie Lea to Fala Flow. And there they take off their boots in the heather, tramp through the lush, damp mosses and dangle their feet in the cool lochan waters.

The larks ascend, the grouse holler, the rushes crinkle, the muirburn snaps.

SONG

She was waiting for a boy
he came skipping down to greet her
through the starch and bleach and buttons
he was singing out her name
the evening clouds are huddled in
so close that you could catch them
granite sheen upon the river
and the shimmering of rain

for miles and miles and miles she'd roam
down Salter's Road to Fala Dam
and all the way home
for miles and miles and miles she'd roam
down Whippielaw and Windy Mains
and all the way home

All the way home
All the way home

All the way home
All the way home
All the way home
All the way home

> *The clatter of geese. A*
> *bright swirling drone.*

SIXTEEN: WE ARE ALL BOG-BORN

> *Crack – crack – go*
> *back – go back – go*
> *back.*

Listen.
It's dusk, and the moorcock cries:

> *go back*
> *go back*
> *go back*

go back to what?
go back to where?

The first place you ever knew
was warm and wild and wet
and in that dark womb you grew.

> *A heart beats.*

We are all bog-born.

> *A dawn light rises.*
> *A blaze of heather*
> *and bog cotton. The*
> *heartbeat rises then*
> *fades.*

Credits

Skippin' Barfit through the Heather, traditional (learned from Alison McMorland)

Up and Awa wi' the Laverock, traditional/Andy Hunter

The Lark in the Clear Air, traditional/Sir Samuel Ferguson (public domain)

Now Westlin Winds, Robert Burns (public domain)

Lungs of Our Land, Karine Polwart

Beo Beo, Karine Polwart

Faultlines, Karine Polwart

The Death of Queen Jane, traditional (learned from Cy Laurie)

Beo Beo Bonnie Bairn o' Mine, traditional (learned from Alison McMorland)

Sphagnum Mass for a Dead Queen, Karine Polwart and Pippa Murphy

Rivers Run, Karine Polwart

Salter's Road, Karine Polwart

STORY

Scene Nine, 'Evergreen', is adapted from 'How the Spruce Became Evergreen', as told by the late Scots Traveller storyteller Duncan Williamson and printed in *Fireside Tales of the Traveller Children* (Canongate Books)

Thanks

To the whole creative team who breathed life into the staging of this piece; to the technical crew at the Royal Lyceum Theatre who supported it; to Rachel Millward at Breathe Festival, and to Ruth Little, for the impetus to conjure an idea in the first place; to David Greig for spotting the potential in this work, and to Alex McGowan for agreeing to put the Lyceum's resources behind it; to Edinburgh International Festival 2016 for its performance platform.

Thanks to Liam Hurley for having my back and turning things around (twice); to Mark Whyles for taking the wheel in so many ways.

To my sources: Dr Brian Moffat, Jude Whitelaw-Smith, Audrey Lees Marchbank, Gus Harper, Alison McMorland, Cy Laurie.

To Meg Kristensen for sharing the story of her grandparents, Will and Roberta Sime, and the birth of her mother, Molly Kristensen.

To Fala Moor and all the life and death in it.

This work is dedicated to the memory of Will and Roberta Sime, Molly Kristensen, Angela Mary Kay Macus, and all the unnamed mothers and healers who have gone before us. It's offered also in gratitude to the maternity and obstetrics staff of Borders General Hospital, for the life of my own children, Arlo and Rosa Foulds.

Bless the NHS. Cherish it.